POETRY PARTY

WRITTEN BY LINDA SPELLMAN
ILLUSTRATED BY BEV ARMSTRONG

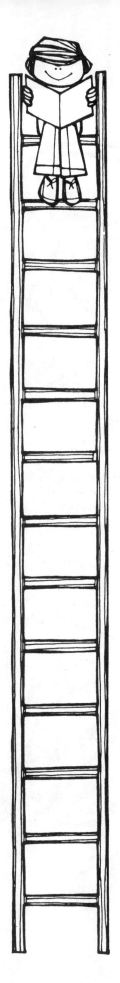

The Learning Works

THIS BOOK BELONGS

TO

_____

The purchase of this book entitles the individual teacher to reproduce copies for use in the classroom.

TABLE OF CONTENTS

POEMS THAT FOLLOW A PATTERN

Name Poem 5
Poetry Patterns 6
Word Patterns 7
Haiku 8-9
Tanka 10-11
Lanterns 12-13
Diamonte 14-15

POEMS THAT RHYME

Rhyme Wheel 16-17
Couplets 18-19
Clerihew 20-21
Quatrains 22-23
Cinquains 24-25
Limericks 26-27
Alliteration 28-29

MISCELLANEOUS POEMS

Parts of Speech Poems 30
Dada 31
Terse Verse 32
ABC Poetry 33
Stair Poems 34
Poetry Mobile 35
My Favorite Poems by Other Poets 36
Poetry Contract 37

POETRY BOOK

The Easy Way to Bind a Book! . . . 38
My Mini-Book of Poetry 39-48

Jeff and Jake

My cats are Jeff and Jake.
They tumble down the stair,
Attacking bags and bugs
and shedding lots of hair!

To the Teacher

This book is designed to help boys and girls in the fourth through the sixth grades have fun with poetry and discover on their own that poems come in all sizes and shapes to express many feelings and fit many moods.

The **Poetry Party** is divided into four sections. The first section, *Poems that Follow a Pattern,* contains simple, nonrhyming poems that follow a predetermined pattern or shape. The second section, *Poems that Rhyme,* is introduced by a rhyme wheel students can assemble and use in structuring their own rhyme schemes. Activities in the third section, entitled *Miscellaneous Poems,* will provide additional creative experiences for your students. The fourth section, *Poetry Book,* is a mini-book in which students can write and illustrate their own poems. You'll find special instructions on how to cover and bind this book on page 38.

In using **Poetry Party** with your class, there are several things to keep in mind. First, when a poetry concept is covered on two pages, it will be more effective to teach both pages at the same time as a mini-unit. Second, reading poetry aloud, talking about rhyme schemes, and having students clap or move in rhythm may make them more sensitive to these essential elements of poetry. Third, even though the book has been written to allow students to work independently, they will derive more from their study of poetry if they share what they have written and learned. Schedule periods for poetry sharing on a regular basis. During these periods, encourage students to read aloud the favorites they have found or written.

The poetry contract on page 37 will help you provide appropriate poetry experiences for all of your students while making allowances for their individual differences. In each contract category, the second choice is geared to the gifted learner.

NAME POEM

A **name poem** is one in which each letter of a person's name (first or first and last) is used as the initial letter for one line of the poem. This type of poem need not rhyme.

Example:

Judy is a teenage girl,
Usually in a social swirl.
Drives her mother up a wall
Yacking on her tenth phone call.

Sean has bright red hair
Even freckles on his face
And he loves to play soccer
Never likes to do chores

On your own: Write poems about yourself and your friends. Illustrate your poems.

Eats almost anything,
Likes to climb a tree,
In overalls and T-shirt
Zany as can be.
Adopting any animal,
Big toe has a blister,
Elizabeth, Elizabeth_
That's my sister!
Hurrah!

POETRY PATTERNS

Poetry patterns are concrete poems written in the shape of the poem's main idea. They do not have to rhyme.

Examples:

WORD PATTERNS

Sometimes one or two words alone can become a form of poetry when written in a form that expresses their meaning.

Examples:

Try making word patterns with some of the words below. Then, create some of your own.

happiness   mirror   sailboat   uneven

jagged   hat

HAIKU

A **haiku** is an unrhymed Japanese poem of three lines containing five, seven, and five syllables, respectively. It is usually light and delicate in feeling and is concerned with something lovely in nature, especially the season of the year. Sometimes, there is a direct contrast within the verse.

Haiku was once part of ancient Japanese courtship rituals. A man would send a haiku to the woman he loved. If she liked the poem, she would write a **tanka** in response.

Structure:
line 1 — five syllables
line 2 — seven syllables
line 3 — five syllables

Example:

Loud, crashing thunder
And then the rain pouring down
The rainbow appears

On your own:

_____

_____

_____

_____

_____

_____

HAIKU

Practice some haiku verse. Then pick your favorite haiku, write it on a half-sheet of paper in your best handwriting, and illustrate it with a delicate watercolor picture.

_____

_____

_____

_____

_____

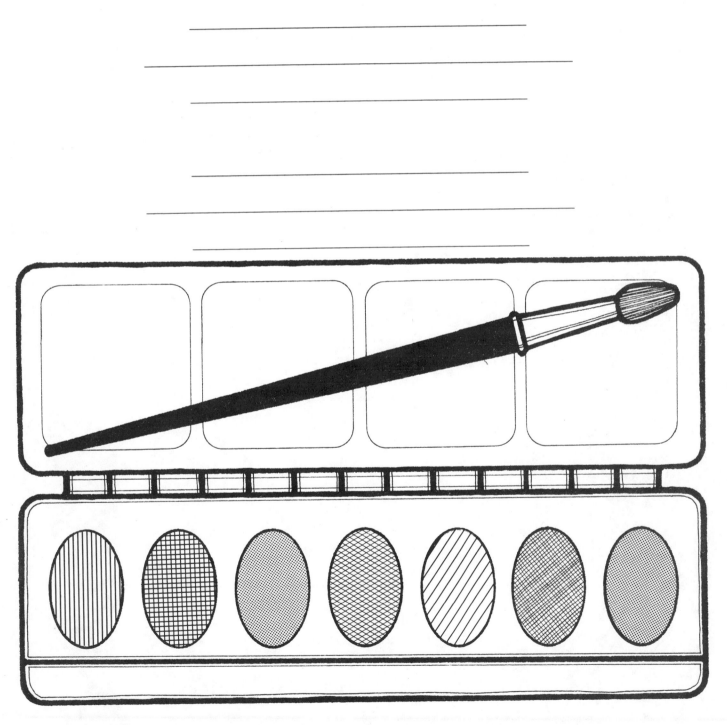

TANKA

Tanka is another oriental verse form much like haiku except that two more lines of seven syllables each are added to give tanka a total of thirty-one syllables.

Structure
  line 1 — five syllables
  line 2 — seven syllables
  line 3 — five syllables
  line 4 — seven syllables
  line 5 — seven syllables

Examples:

The gate is unlocked.
Boys and girls with shiny shoes
And full lunch boxes
Gather to talk of summer
While they listen for the bell.

The great out-of-doors
Beckoned to us one and all
We sought nature's joys
Along her creeks and rivers
And in the cool of the glade.

On your own:

_____

_____

_____

_____

_____

_____

_____

_____

TANKA

Practice writing the old courtship form of tanka. First, write the haiku. Then write the tanka response. You may make the poems in the form of friendship notes from one person to another.

haiku note

tanka response

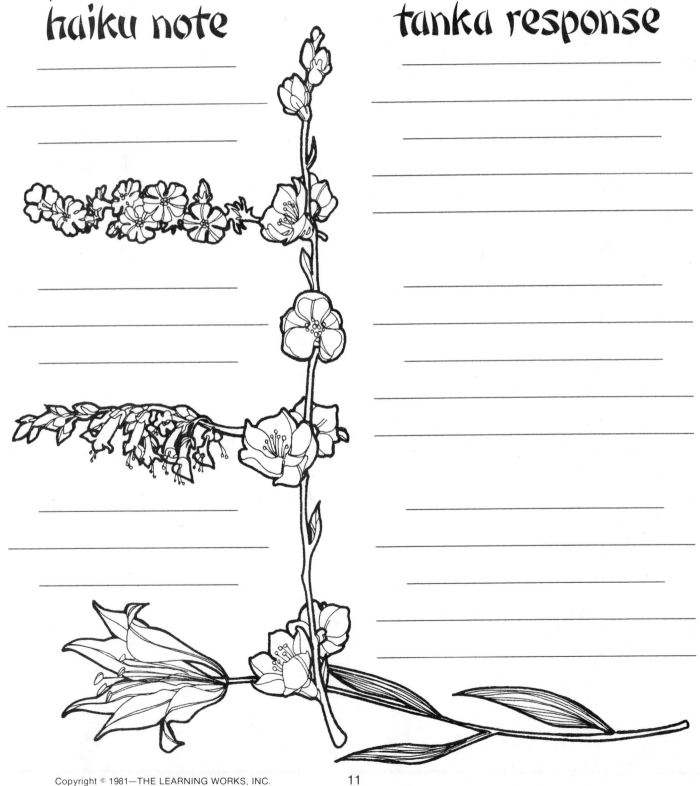

11

LANTERNS

A **lantern** is a light and airy Japanese poem that is written in the shape of a Japanese lantern. Lanterns can be written singly or in a string as illustrated below.

Structure:
line 1 — one syllable
line 2 — two syllables
line 3 — three syllables
line 4 — four syllables
line 5 — one syllable

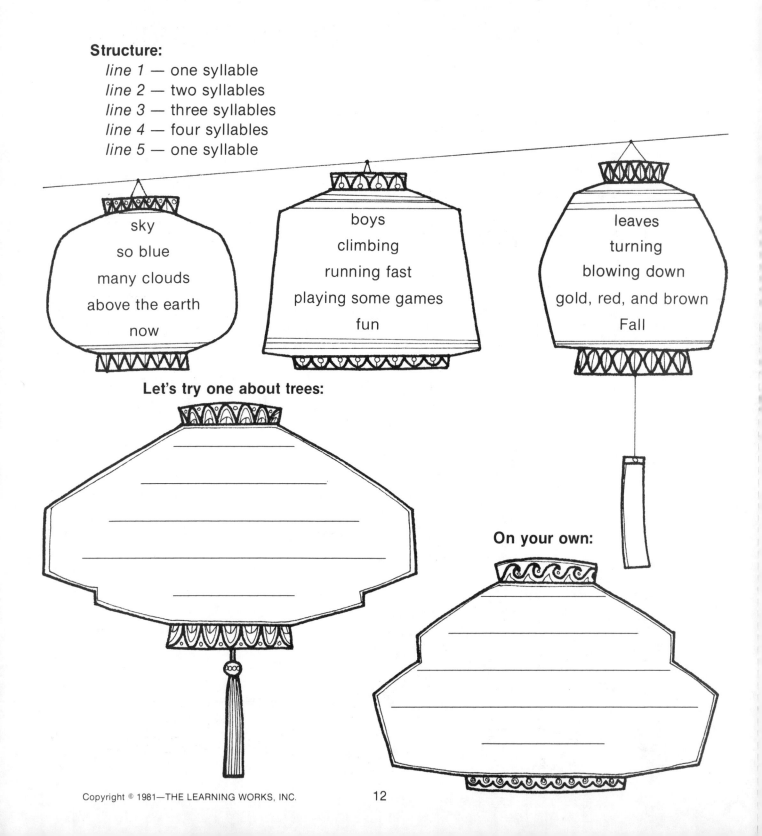

sky
so blue
many clouds
above the earth
now

boys
climbing
running fast
playing some games
fun

leaves
turning
blowing down
gold, red, and brown
Fall

Let's try one about trees:

On your own:

12

LANTERNS

Write lanterns for the patterns below. Color each of the patterns a different color, cut them out, and hang them up.

13

DIAMONTE

The **diamonte** is fun and easy to write. The purpose is to go from the subject at the top of the diamond to another totally different (and sometimes opposite) subject at the bottom.

Structure:
    line 1 — one noun (subject #1)
    line 2 — two adjectives (describing subject #1)
    line 3 — three participles (ending in —*ing,* telling about subject #1)
    line 4 — four nouns (first two related to subject #1, second two related to subject #2)
    line 5 — three participles (about subject #2)
    line 6 — two adjectives (describing subject #2)
    line 7 — one noun (subject #2)

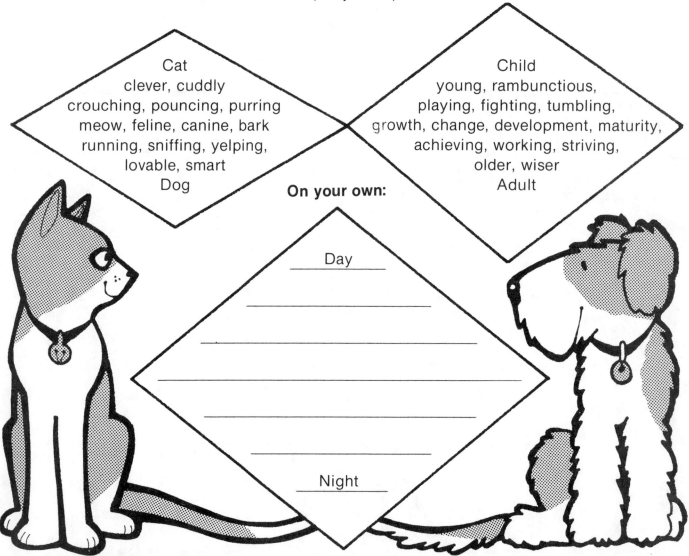

Cat
clever, cuddly
crouching, pouncing, purring
meow, feline, canine, bark
running, sniffing, yelping,
lovable, smart
Dog

Child
young, rambunctious,
playing, fighting, tumbling,
growth, change, development, maturity,
achieving, working, striving,
older, wiser
Adult

On your own:

____ Day ____

_____

_____

_____

_____

____ Night ____

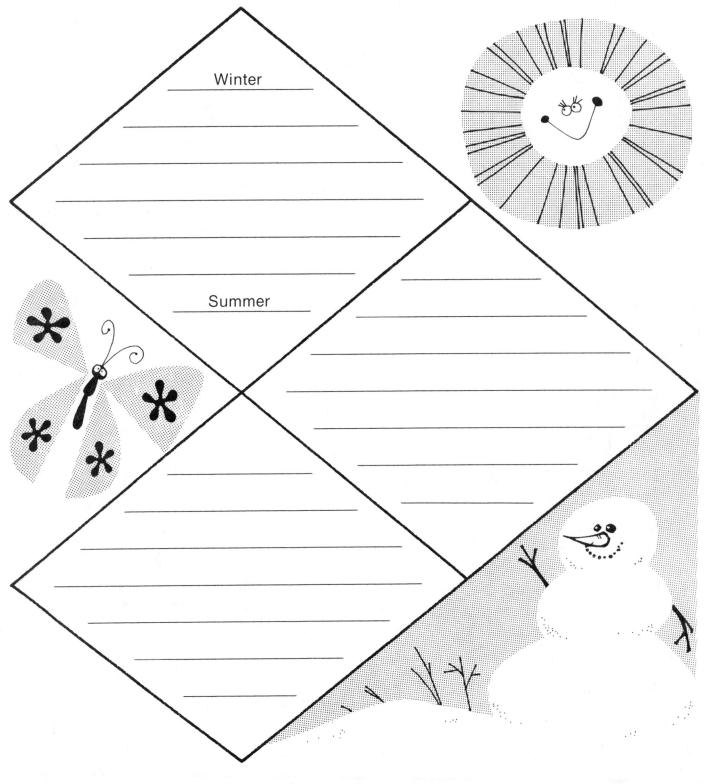

Name _____

DIAMONTE

Practice writing diamontes. The first one has been started for you. Rewrite one of your favorite diamontes on another sheet of paper and illustrate it.

Winter
_____
_____
_____
_____

Summer
_____

_____
_____
_____
_____

_____
_____
_____
_____

RHYME WHEEL

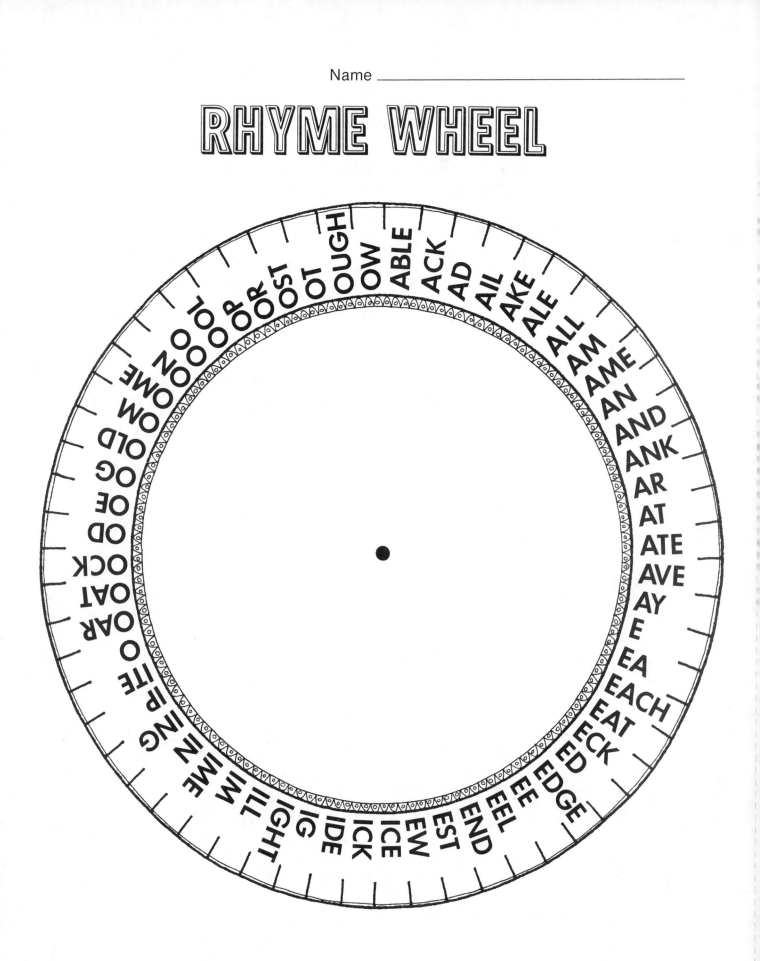

16

Name _____

You can use the rhyme wheel to help you write more interesting poetry. Remember, though, that this wheel includes only a few of the words you can use for rhyming.

Directions: Cut out both wheels. Place the smaller wheel on the top, center it, and put a brad through the center circle of both wheels.

brad

17

COUPLETS

The simplest rhymed pattern is the **couplet**, which consists of two rhyming lines. They are usually written with a humorous twist. The lines can be of any length, but the rhythm and the rhyme should match the thought or mood of the poem.

YEEK!

Examples:

The teacher called the students in,
Then wished she could escape the din.

My son, Jonathan, came running out
To see what the noise was all about.

Jack and Jill went up the hill
So their bucket they could fill.

On your own:

_____

_____

_____

_____

_____

_____

_____

COUPLETS

Write some more couplets, but this time make them tell a story so that, when you finish, you will have one long poem. Give your poem a title.

_____

_____

_____

_____

_____

_____

_____

_____

_____

_____

_____

_____

_____

_____

_____

The spider dangles, legs a-wiggle, and grins a little spider giggle.
She sees a fast-approaching fly, and plans to bake it in a pie.

CLERIHEW

The **clerihew** is a four-line poem that makes a brief, humorous statement about a person. It is named after Edmund Clerihew Bentley (1875-1956), an English writer of detective stories who originated this verse form.

Structure:

line 1 — ends with a person's name
line 2 — rhymes with line 1
lines 3 and 4 — rhyme with each other

Examples:
Little Mary Jane
Sittin' in the rain,
Lost her red raincoat
And soon will be afloat!

Down the street goes big Bob Brown
Tallest kid around this town
Six foot eight is his new size
Towers o'er the other guys.

On your own:

_____

_____

_____

_____

_____

_____

_____

CLASS CLERIHEW

This is a fun way to cover a classroom bulletin board or make a class mini-book. Use the spaces below to write clerihews about your classmates—but no put-downs, please.

Arrange your collection on a bulletin board or in a mini-book, making sure you have at least one clerihew for each person.

21

QUATRAINS

Quatrains are four-line poems that may follow any one of four different rhyme patterns (AABB, ABAB, ABBA, or ABCB).

When quatrains are combined to make a long poem, each group of four lines is called a **stanza**. Stanzas are the "paragraphs" of poetry.

Quatrains are used in ballads to tell a story, sometimes humorous, but more often sad.

Examples:

ABCB The rushing ocean waves
       Beat harshly on the sand.
    They roar and crash and foam
       As they break upon the land.

ABAB On one dark and wintry day
       When it was very cold,
   Down flew a screaming jay
       Squawking in a voice so bold.

On your own: Try writing quatrains in each of these rhyme patterns.

AABB _____

_____

_____

ABAB _____

_____

_____

ABCB _____

_____

_____

Name _____

QUATRAINS

Write a quatrain in an ABBA pattern.

_____

_____

_____

_____

Cut a picture from a magazine. Paste it on another piece of paper, and write two or three stanzas of quatrains in any rhyme pattern about it.

_____

_____

_____

_____

_____

_____

_____

_____

_____

_____

CINQUAINS

The **cinquain** is a simple, five-line verse form. Its structure follows specific rules.

Structure:

line 1 — one word of two syllables (may be the title)
line 2 — four syllables (describing the subject or title)
line 3 — six syllables (showing action)
line 4 — eight syllables (expressing a feeling or observation about the subject)
line 5 — two syllables (describing or renaming the subject)

Examples:

Kittens
Frisky, playful
Mewing, jumping, bouncing
Creep silently on padded paws
Mischief

Mountain
Isolated
Snow-capped and cloud-touching
White against shining, azure sky
High peak

On your own:

_____

_____

_____

_____

_____

_____

_____

Name _____

CINQUAINS

Practice writing more cinquains using the illustrations on this page as your topics.

_____

_____

_____

_____

_____

_____

_____

LIMERICKS

A **limerick** is a humorous five-line poem that follows a definite rhyme pattern and has a particular rhythm.

Just as music is written in groups of notes called **measures**, poetry is written in groups of syllables called **feet**. A foot usually contains several unstressed syllables but only one stressed syllable. A particular verse form gets its characteristic rhythm, beat, or **meter** from the number of unstressed syllables and the position of the stressed syllable in each foot, and from the number of feet in each line.

In the limerick, each foot contains one or two unstressed syllables followed by one that is stressed. There must be three of these feet in each of the first two lines, two in each of the second two lines, and three again in the last line.

Structure:

Lines 1, 2, and 5 each have three feet (that is, three stressed, or accented, syllables) and rhyme with one another (A).

Lines 3 and 4 each have only two feet (that is, two stressed, or accented, syllables) and rhyme with each other (B). These two lines are always indented.

Example: Read the poem aloud, noting the rhyme pattern and which syllables are stressed. Syllables marked with a ◡ are unstressed. Syllables marked with a ◢ are stressed. Vertical lines separate the feet.

3 feet	There once | was a boy | at our school |	A
3 feet	Who thought | he was ter | ribly cool. |	A
2 feet, indented	He wore | fancy jeans |	B
2 feet, indented	Strode around | with the teens |	B
3 feet	But end | ed up play | ing the fool. |	A

Say the poem aloud one more time. This time, clap the rhythm. Try to feel the rhythm of the limerick. Now write a limerick of your own:

There was an old _____ from _____

Who liked to _____ on a _____

_____

_____

26

LIMERICKS

Practice some more limericks. Remember that lines 1, 2, and 5 have three feet and rhyme, while lines 3 and 4 have two feet and rhyme.

There once was a girl who loved bugs

And kept them in jars, cups, and jugs.

WES WALKINGSTICK

BOWSER BEETLE

AMANDA ANT

She tickled their shins, scratched under their chins,

And carefully gave them all hugs.

ALLITERATION

Alliteration is the repetition of a sound in two or more neighboring words. It is the repeated use of an accented syllable that has the same beginning sound, as in "Peter Piper picked a peck of pickled peppers . . . ."

Examples:

Alice **a**te **a**n **a**lligator.

Henry **h**ad a **h**ank of **h**air.

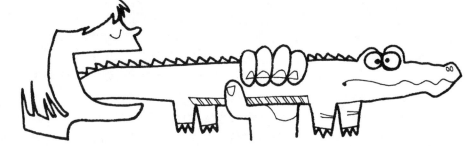

On your own: Write a four- to six-line poem using the *same* sound to start as many words as possible. Try to rhyme the even-numbered lines.

line 1 _____

line 2 _____

line 3 _____

line 4 _____

line 5 _____

line 6 _____

Now write a four-line poem (quatrain) with an ABAB pattern. Use the *same* sound to start as many words as possible.

_____

_____

_____

_____

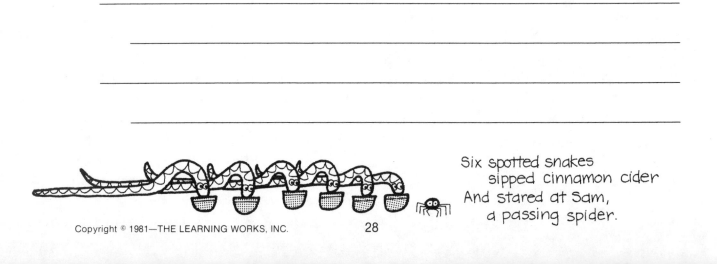

Six spotted snakes
  sipped cinnamon cider
And stared at Sam,
  a passing spider.

28

Name _____

ALLITERATION

Alaric Alexander Watts (1797-1864), an English journalist and poet, wrote the poem, "The Siege of Belgrade," in which every line uses alliteration. All the words in line I begin with the letter A, in line 2 with the letter B, and so on through the entire alphabet. Apparently, Watts had trouble with the letter J, for that was the only letter he omitted.

On your own: Try completing this type of poem by using the same beginning letter for every word in the row. Be sure your poem makes sense.

Alex _____ alike,

Borrowed _____ bike

_____ clue

_____ drew

Now, continue this poem or write a similar poem of your own. Remember to use an AABBCCDD rhyme pattern.

_____

_____

_____

_____

_____

_____

_____

Big, bad Barney Bat
Calmly chased Clarissa Cat.

PARTS OF SPEECH POEMS

These poems are fun to write and offer a chance to practice using parts of speech.

Structure:

line 1 — one article (a, an, the) + one noun
line 2 — one adjective + one conjunction (joining word) + one adjective
line 3 — one verb + one conjunction + one verb
line 4 — one adverb
line 5 — one noun (relating to the noun in the first line)

Examples:

A painting,
    colorful and exciting,
Decorates and fulfills
    aesthetically.
Art.

The cliff,
    sharp and rocky,
Juts and looms
    above.
Wall.

On your own:

_____

_____

_____

_____

_____

_____

_____

_____

_____

_____

_____

_____

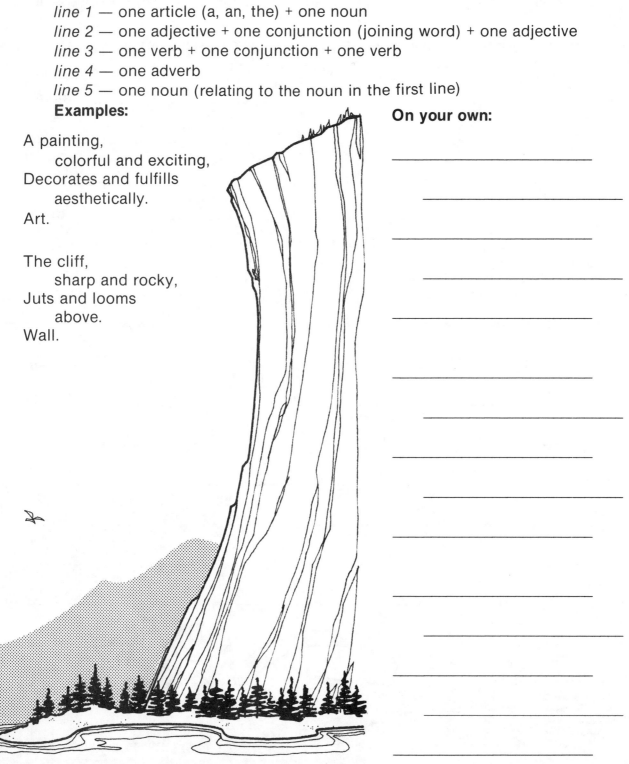

DADA

Dada has to be easiest poetry to write! You just follow the directions below.

Originally Dada poetry was written by artists and poets in Paris, France, who clipped words from newspapers, scrambled them, and then arranged them in lines to form nonsense poems.

Structure:

1. Write down ten verbs, eight nouns, and some pronouns on small pieces of paper.

2. Jumble them up in a bowl and draw them out one at a time.

3. Arrange the words on a piece of paper until you like the way they look.

Have fun! Try some:

firecracker   nibble
snore   a   tickle
juggle   jellyfish
purr   a   pickle
balloon   a   squish
platypus   hiccup   kazoo
hug   away   the   flu

31

TERSE VERSE

Terse verse is a short poem with a very long title or introduction. The introduction is made up of big, impressive-sounding words, and the poem contains some rhyming words.

Examples:

What Mary was given when her brother turned her around:
    A sister twister.

What Jeff did in preparation for reciting his poem:
    Rehearse the verse.

On your own:

_____
_____
_____
_____

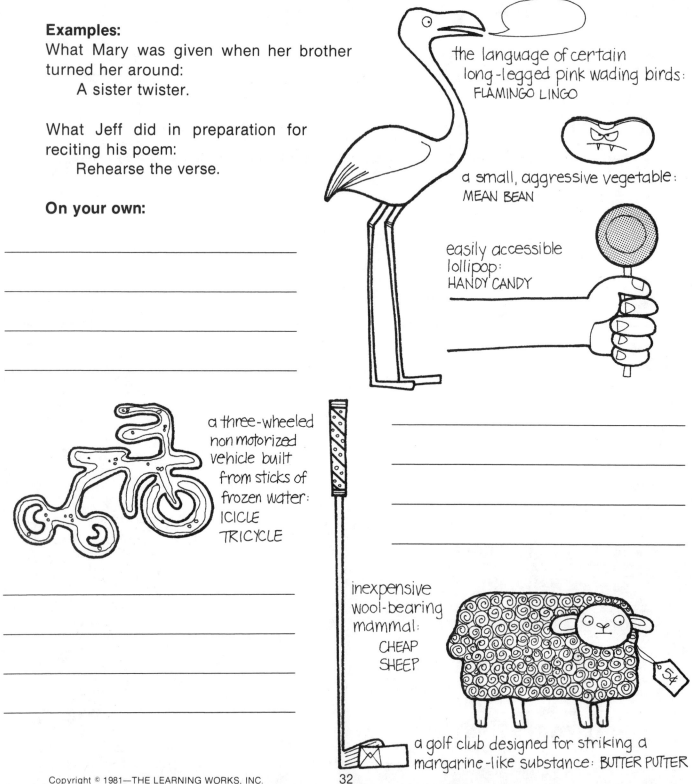

the language of certain long-legged pink wading birds: FLAMINGO LINGO

a small, aggressive vegetable: MEAN BEAN

easily accessible lollipop: HANDY CANDY

a three-wheeled non motorized vehicle built from sticks of frozen water: ICICLE TRICYCLE

inexpensive wool-bearing mammal: CHEAP SHEEP

a golf club designed for striking a margarine-like substance: BUTTER PUTTER

ABC POETRY

ABC poetry is written in a short form and expresses strong emotion.

Structure:

The first four lines are clauses expressing an emotion.

The initial letters of the beginning words in each line are written alphabetically. (The first line does not have to begin with A.)

Line 5 is a sentence beginning with any letter.

Examples:

Afraid
Because I
Cannot see
Down the hall—
What could that noise be?

Entirely happy
Finally got an A
Going to a party
Have a new friend
What a wonderful day!

On your own:

_____

_____

_____

_____

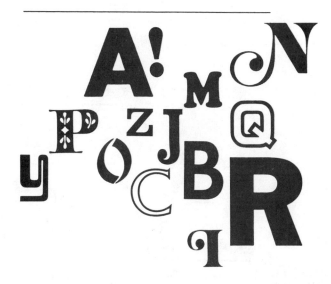

_____

_____

_____

_____

_____

_____

_____

Name _____

STAIR POEMS

A stair poem is one in which the ideas build up following a stair pattern.

Structure:

step 1 — the topic or main idea (usually one word)

step 2 — three adjectives describing the topic

step 3 — a place or time connected with the topic

step 4 — a summarization of the topic or a phrase which means the same as the topic

Example:

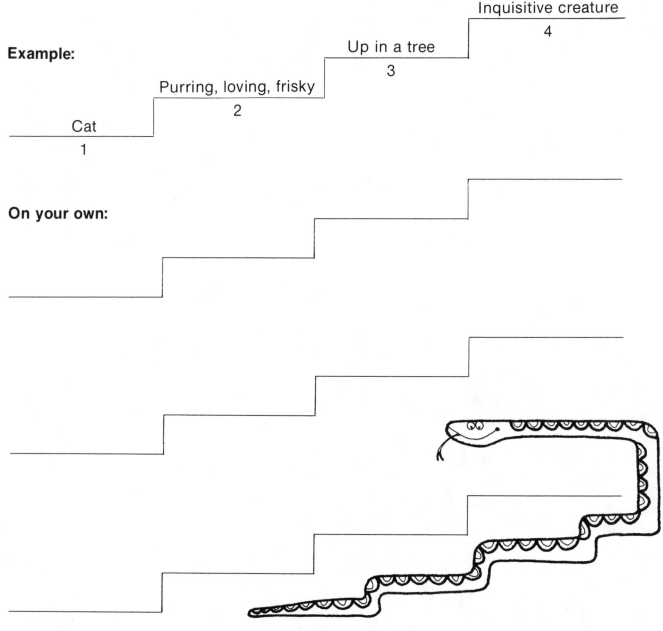

Inquisitive creature
4

Up in a tree
3

Purring, loving, frisky
2

Cat
1

On your own:

POETRY MOBILE

A **poetry mobile** is an artistic method of illustrating the rhythm and meter of poetry. Mobiles are made up of words and short phrases placed on cardboard patterns and allowed to hang free in the air.

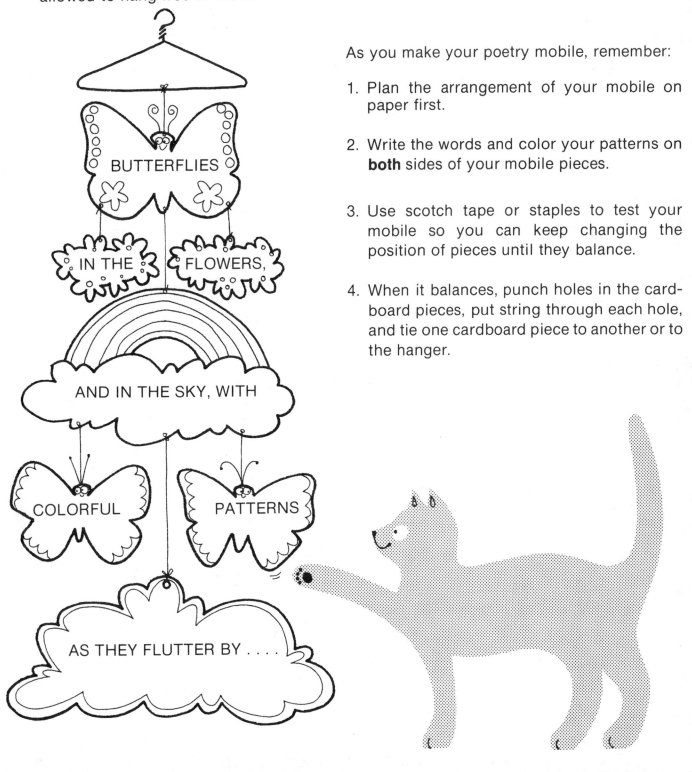

As you make your poetry mobile, remember:

1. Plan the arrangement of your mobile on paper first.

2. Write the words and color your patterns on **both** sides of your mobile pieces.

3. Use scotch tape or staples to test your mobile so you can keep changing the position of pieces until they balance.

4. When it balances, punch holes in the cardboard pieces, put string through each hole, and tie one cardboard piece to another or to the hanger.

BUTTERFLIES

IN THE   FLOWERS,

AND IN THE SKY, WITH

COLORFUL   PATTERNS

AS THEY FLUTTER BY . . . .

MY FAVORITE POEMS BY OTHER POETS

POETRY CONTRACT

Complete the areas that are marked with a ✔.

Poetry Packet

☐ Write each of the different kinds of poems as they are assigned. After they have been checked and returned to you, keep them in your poetry folder.

☐ Select a theme and write it on the line below. Use this same theme when you write each of the different kinds of poems as they are assigned. After they have been checked and returned to you, keep them in your poetry folder. (**Examples of themes**: winter, beauty, love, animals, trees, trucks, birds, etc.)

My theme is _____

Poetry Appreciation

☐ Using poetry books, find five poems that you really enjoy reading. Copy them exactly as the author has written them. Include the title and the author's name. Keep them in your poetry folder.

☐ Using poetry books, find five poems that have your chosen theme. Copy them exactly as the author has written them. Include the title and the author's name. Keep them in your poetry folder.

Poetry Recitation

☐ Choose a poem from your collection to *memorize!* Be prepared to recite your poem to the class.

☐ Choose a poem from your collection to *memorize*. Record your poem on tape, being sure to include your name and the author's name. Speak clearly and with expression. Then recite the poem you have chosen to the class.

Poem Book

☐ Write your poems on the pages of the mini-book of poetry. Illustrate the poems and then bind the pages together.

☐ Using your choice of book size and shape, write your poems in a book form. Illustrate your poems, and bind them together, adding a hard cover.

THE EASY WAY TO BIND A BOOK!

1. Choose a paper size. Determine the number of pages you will need. Cut two pieces of colored construction paper the same size as the book paper. If you are making the mini-book, duplicate the pages back-to-back in the same order as they are printed in this book. Cut the duplicated pages in half horizontally, and place them in the correct numerical order. Add two sheets of construction paper the same size (5½ x 8½").

2. Fold the pages of the book in half, keeping both sheets of construction paper on the outside.

3. Using a sewing machine, stitch the book pages and construction paper together down the middle, leaving at least 3 inches of thread free at both the top and the bottom. Tie off the thread at both ends and clip the thread.

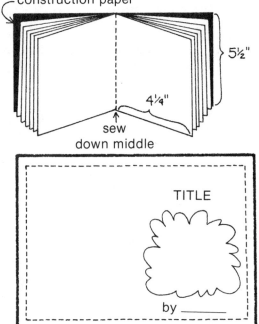

4. Cut two pieces of cardboard the size of your folded book plus ⅜" added to each dimension (4⅝" x 5⅞").

5. Cut a large sheet of paper the size of your original pages before you folded them (step 2) plus 2" each way (7½" x 10½"). Leave a 1" margin all the way around the paper. Draw your illustration and title on the right-hand side. Laminate or cover with clear plastic adhesive.

6. Turn your cover over. Place the two cardboard pieces ⅜" apart and centered on the inside of the cover. Rubber cement or glue them in place. Trim and miter the corners and rubber cement them in place.

7. Place rubber cement or glue on the outside sheet of construction paper on your book, and carefully press your book into the inside of the cover.

Cut off corners carefully.

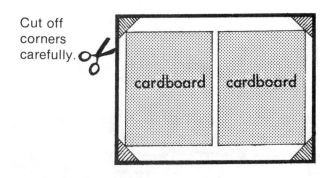

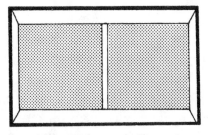

Fold over the edges and cement them in place.

My Mini-Book of Poetry

MORE FAVORITE POEMS...

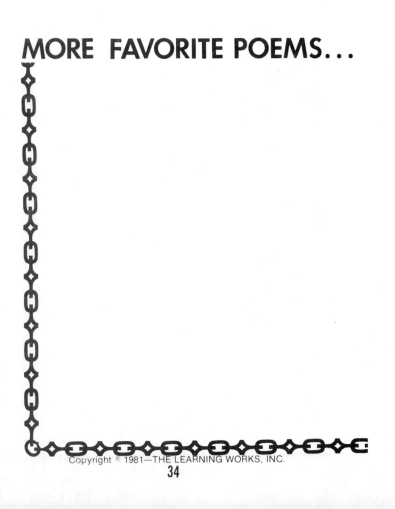

CONTENTS

Haiku 2, 3

Tanka 4, 5

Diamonte 6, 7

Parts of Speech Poems 8, 9

Alliteration 10, 11

Couplets 12, 13

Quatrains 14, 15

Cinquains 16, 17

Limericks 18, 19

Lanterns 20, 21

Poetry Patterns 22, 23

This book is
dedicated to

_____

Published by
Kids Learning, Ltd.
19____

Word Patterns 24

Clerihew 25

Dada 26

Terse Verse 27

ABC Poetry 28

Stair Poems 29

Name Poems 30-31

My Favorite Poems
  by Other Poets 32-33

More Favorite Poems
  by Other Poets 34-35

MY FAVORITE POEMS... □□□□

Poetry is wonderful
Exciting as can be.
Here are some poems
Written just by me.

32

1

NAME POEMS 🔲🔲🔲🔲

Haiku

30

3

Haiku

2

NAME POEMS

31

Tanka

STAIR POEMS

4

29

ABC POETRY

abcdefghijklmnopq

28

DADA

26

Tanka

5

DIAMONTE

7

DIAMONTE

6

TERSE VERSE

27

Parts of Speech

nouns pronouns verbs

CLERIHEW

8

25

WORD PATTERNS

Poems

adjectives and adverbs

24

9

POETRY

Alliteration

22

11

Alliteration

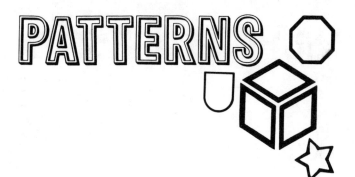

PATTERNS

10

23

COUPLETS

12

21

L A N T

20

COUPLETS

13

LIMERICKS

18

Quatrains

15

Quatrains

LIMERICKS

14

19

CINQUAINS

16

17